ASL

This number tracing activity book with the basics of
American Sign Language (ASL) for Kids, and it's AMAZING.
The book has meaningful activities to put your sign language
knowledge into practice.
The illustrations are beautiful and easy to understand for kids.
The best way to become a good sign language speaker and
to master writing of numbers 0-10 is to practice,
and this book will help you do that.
American Sign Language is an amazing visual language
that uses our hands,
facial expressions, and body language to express ourselves
to those who have difficulty hearing or speaking.
Sign language is not just for the deaf or hard of hearing
-it is for anyone who wants to become a more skilled communicator

© Copyright 2021 - All rights reserved.

The content contained within this book may not be reproduced, duplicated or transmitted without direct written permission from the author or the publisher.

Under no circumstances will any blame or legal responsibility be held against the publisher, or author, for any damages, reparation, or monetary loss due to the information contained within this book. Either directly or indirectly. You are responsible for your own choices, actions, and results.

Legal Notice:

This book is copyright protected. This book is only for personal use. You cannot amend, distribute, sell, use, quote or paraphrase any part, or the content within this book, without the consent of the author or publisher.
Some pictures "Designed by Freepik"

Disclaimer Notice:

Please note the information contained within this document is for educational and entertainment purposes only. All effort has been executed to present accurate, up to date, and reliable, complete information. No warranties of any kind are declared or implied. Readers acknowledge that the author is not engaging in the rendering of legal, financial, medical or professional advice. The content within this book has been derived from various sources. Please consult a licensed professional before attempting any techniques outlined in this book.

By reading this document, the reader agrees that under no circumstances is the author responsible for any losses, direct or indirect, which are incurred as a result of the use of the information contained within this document, including, but not limited to, — errors, omissions, or inaccuracies.

ARE YOU READY FOR
NUMBER TRACING PRACTICE
WITH SIGN LANGUAGE?

LET'S GO!

WE'LL START WITH A TUTORIAL...

TRACING LINES AND LERNING SHAPES

START AT THE CIRCLE 1

FOLLOW THE ARROWS AND TRACE THE DOTTED LINE

END AT THE STOP SIGN

TRACE WITH YOUR FINGER

THEN TRACE WITH A CRAYON

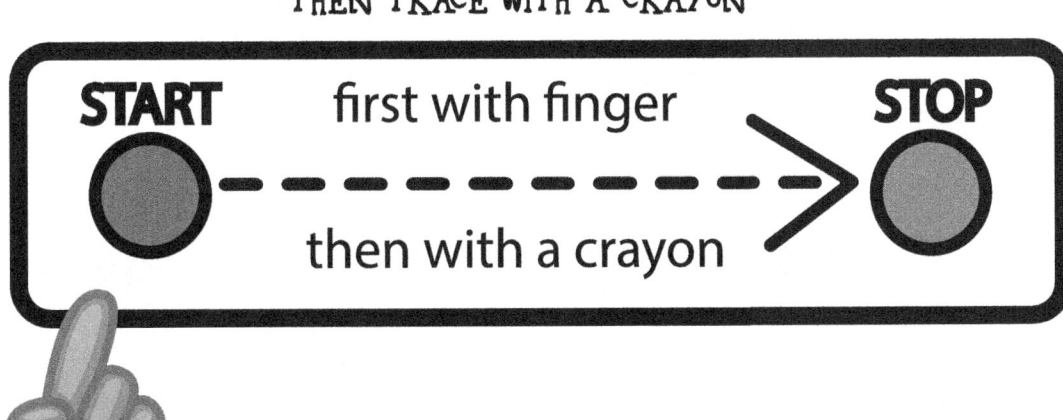

START first with finger **STOP**
- - - - - - - ->
then with a crayon

THE CORRECT WAY TO HOLD A PEN

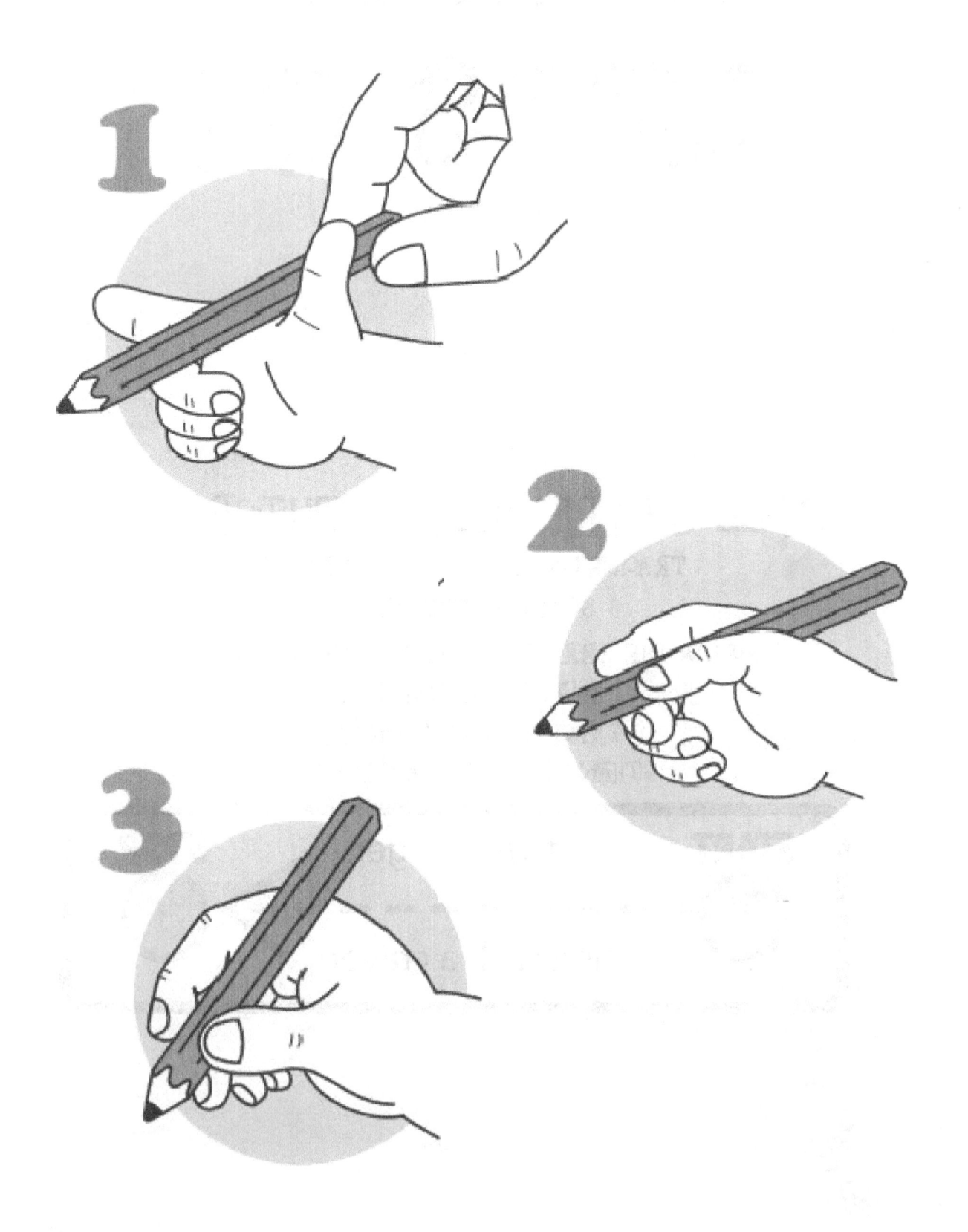

1

2

3

ASL

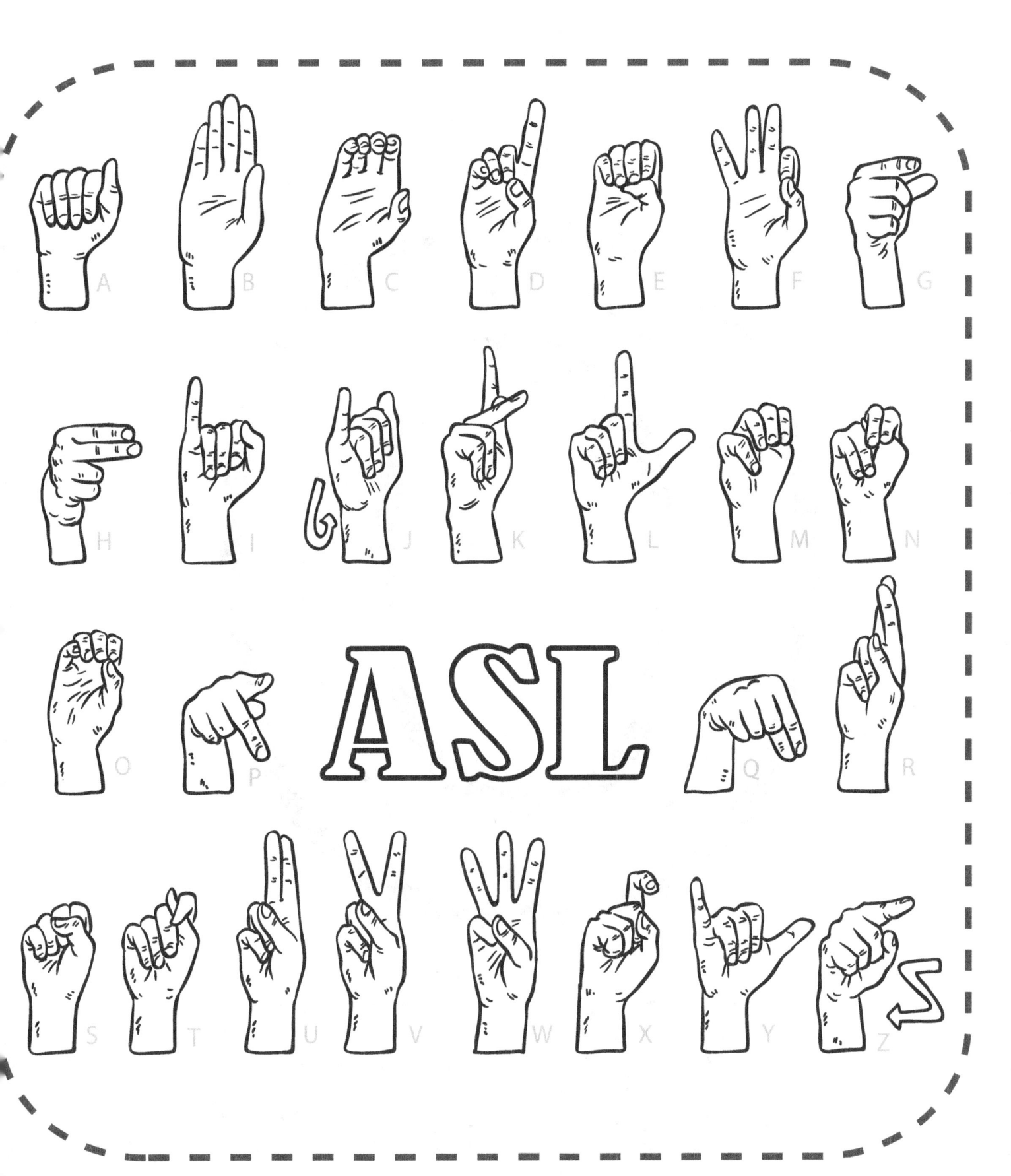

A B C D E F G
H I J K L M N
O P Q R
S T U V W X Y Z

O

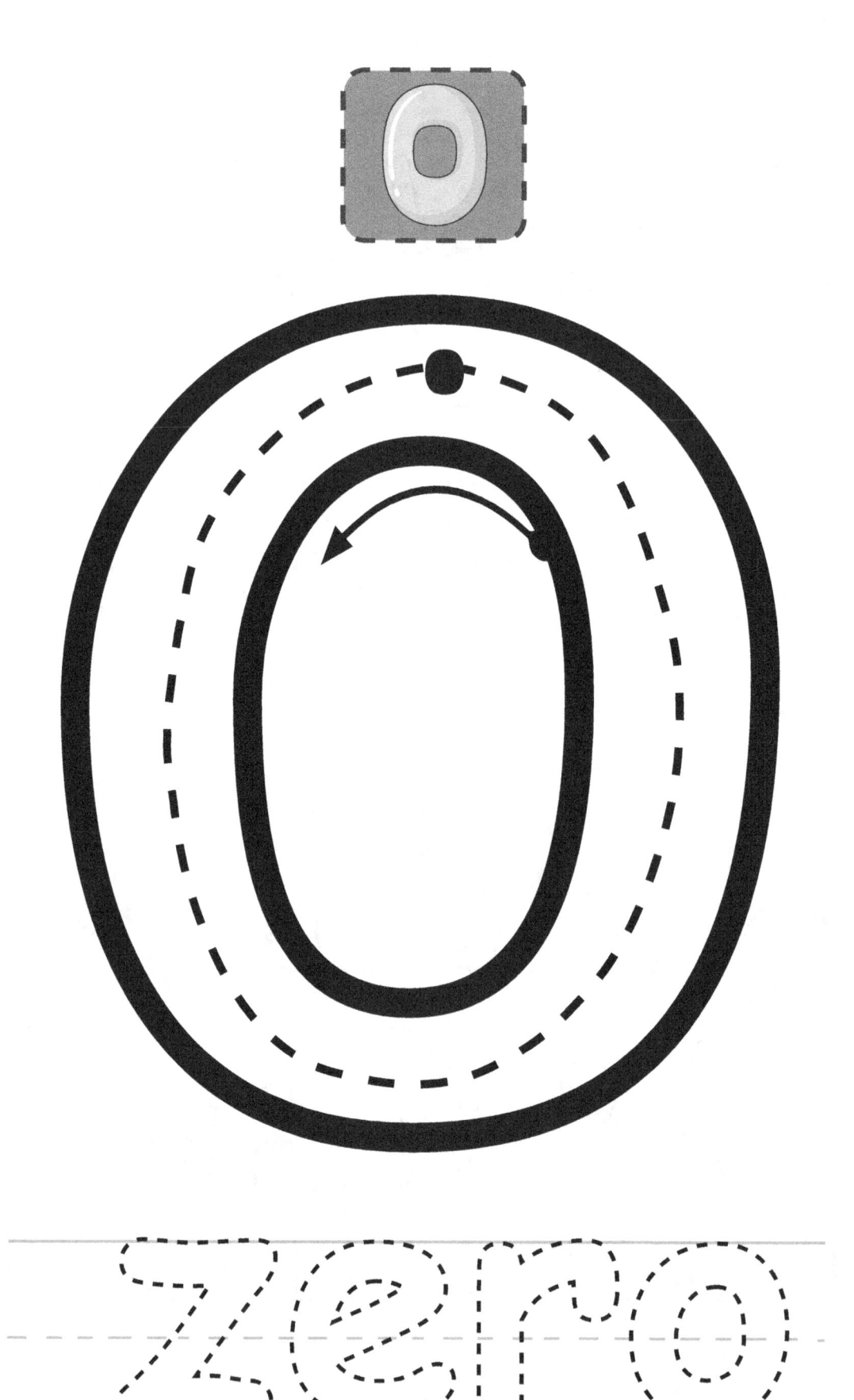

zero

zero

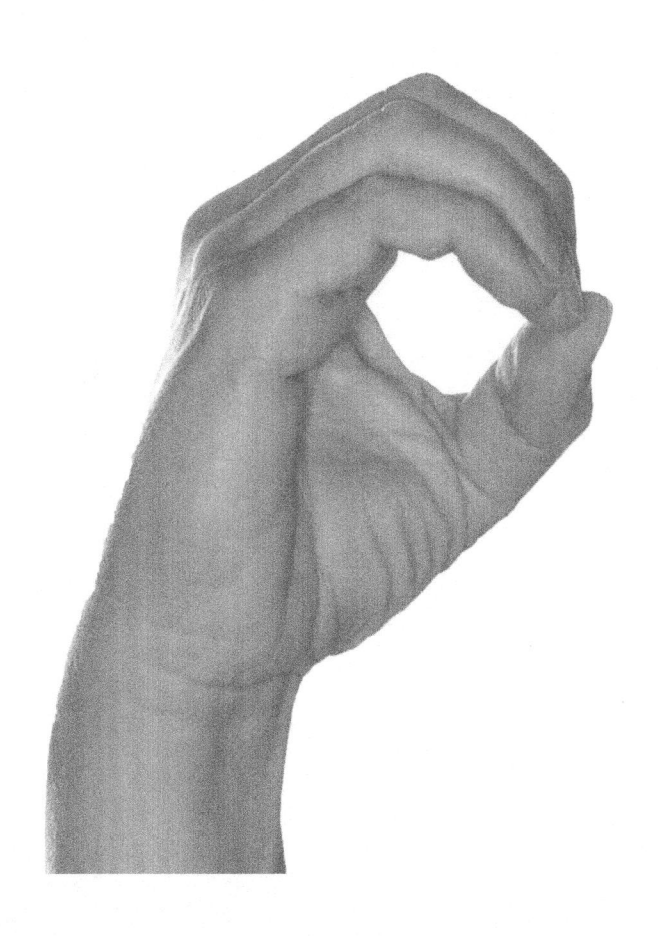

o

zero zero

zero zero zero

zero zero zero

0

1

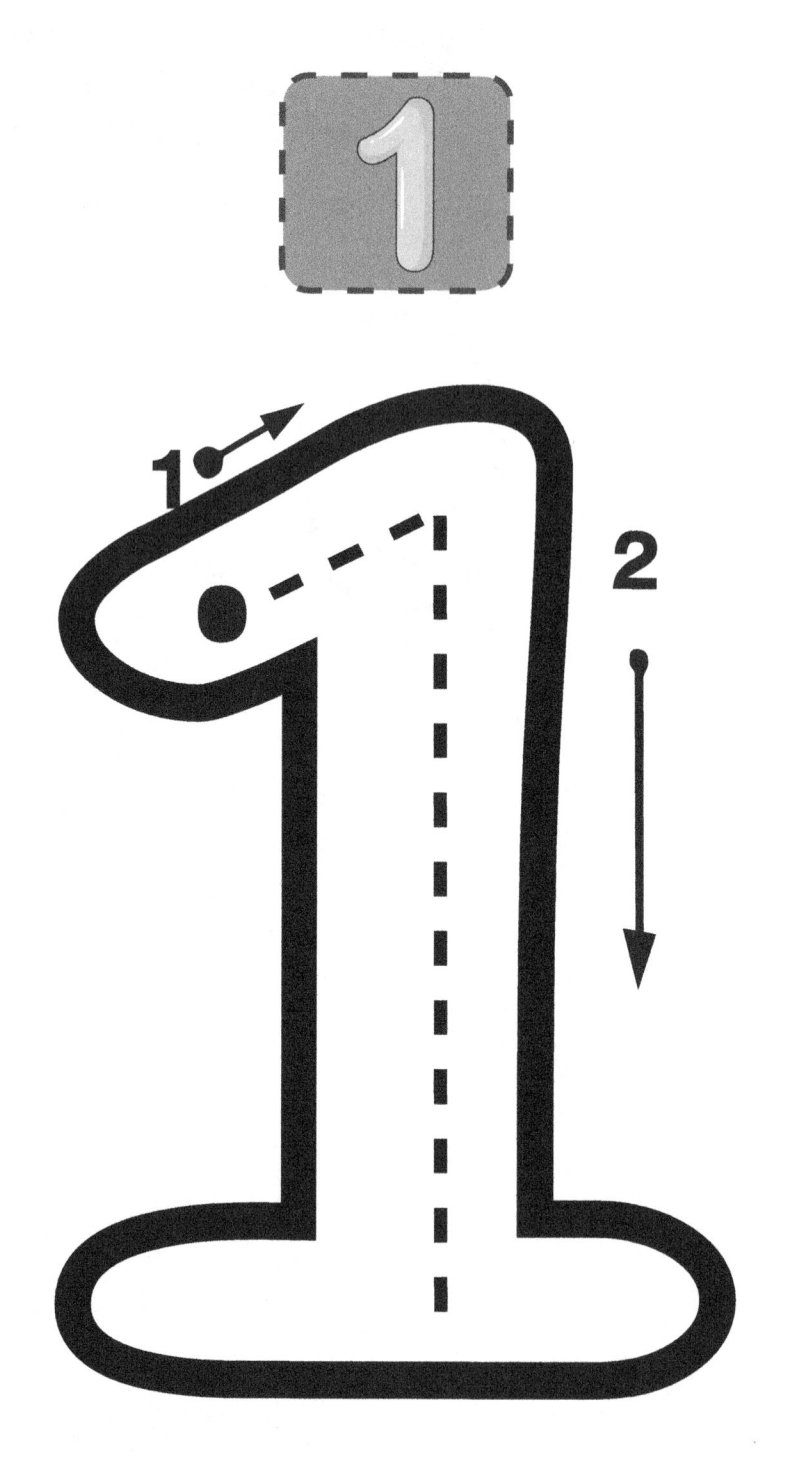

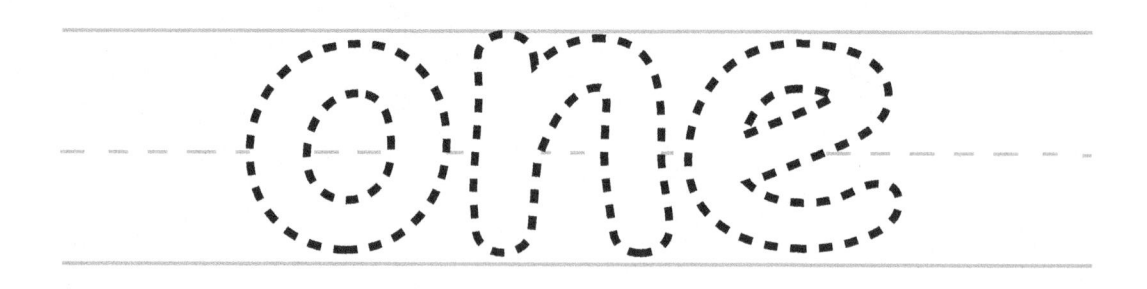

one

one

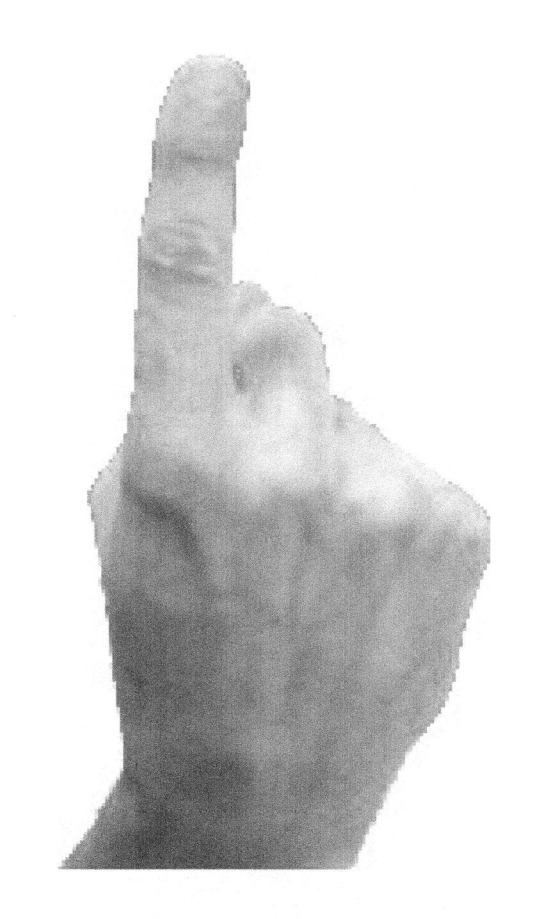

1

one one

one one one

one one one

1

2

two

two

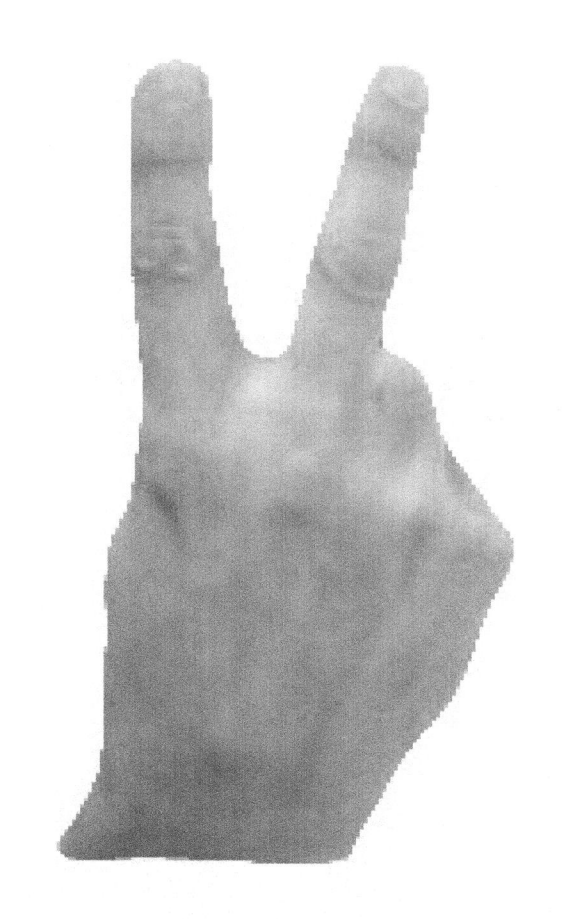

2

two two two

two two two

two two two

2

3

three

three

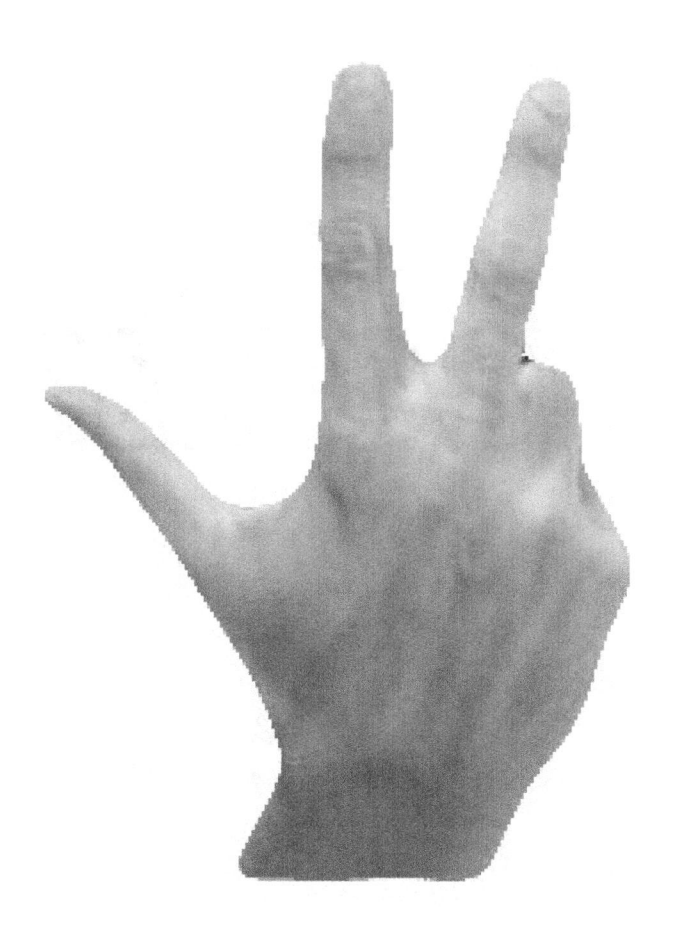

3

three three

three three

three three

3

3 3 3 3 3 3 3 3 3

4

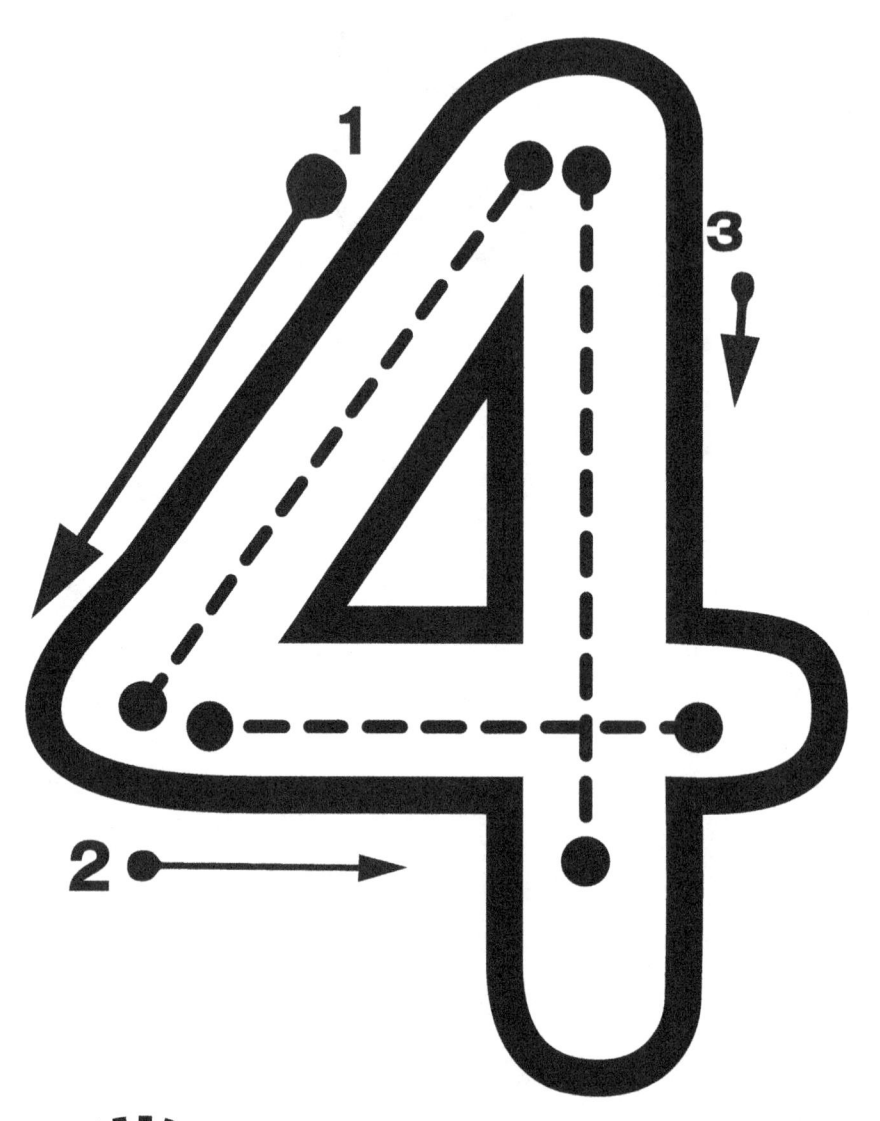

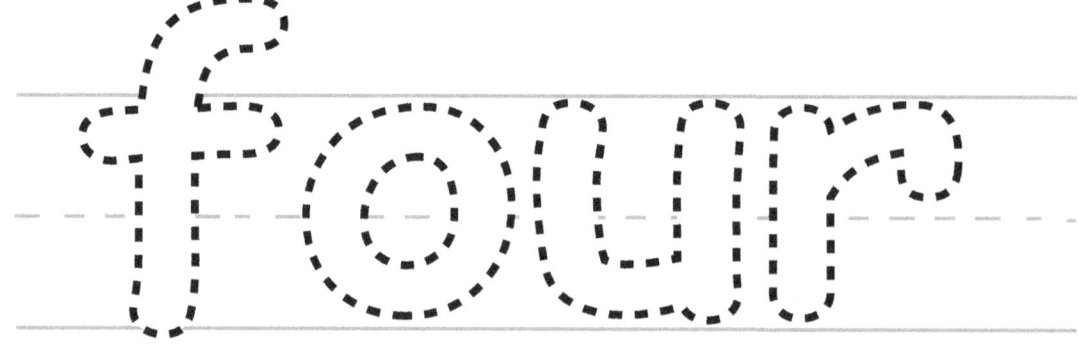

four

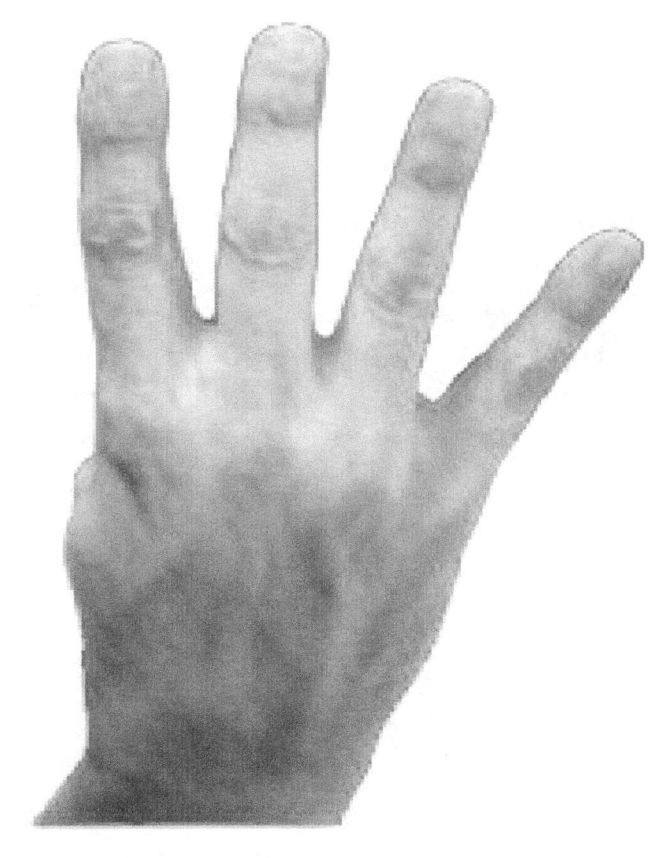

four

4

four four

four four

four four

4

5

five

five

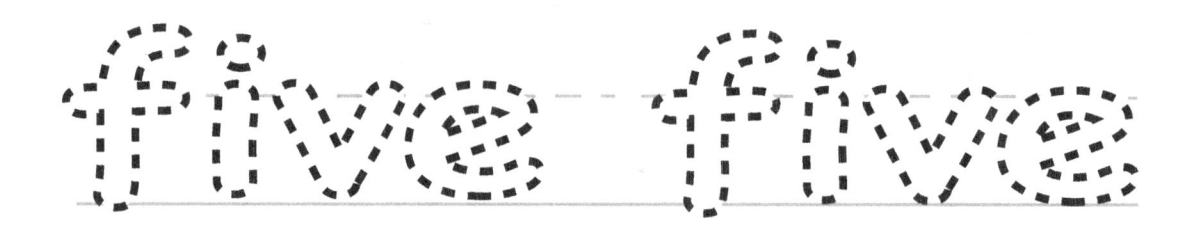

5

five five

five five

five five

5

5 5 5 5 5 5 5 5 5 5

6

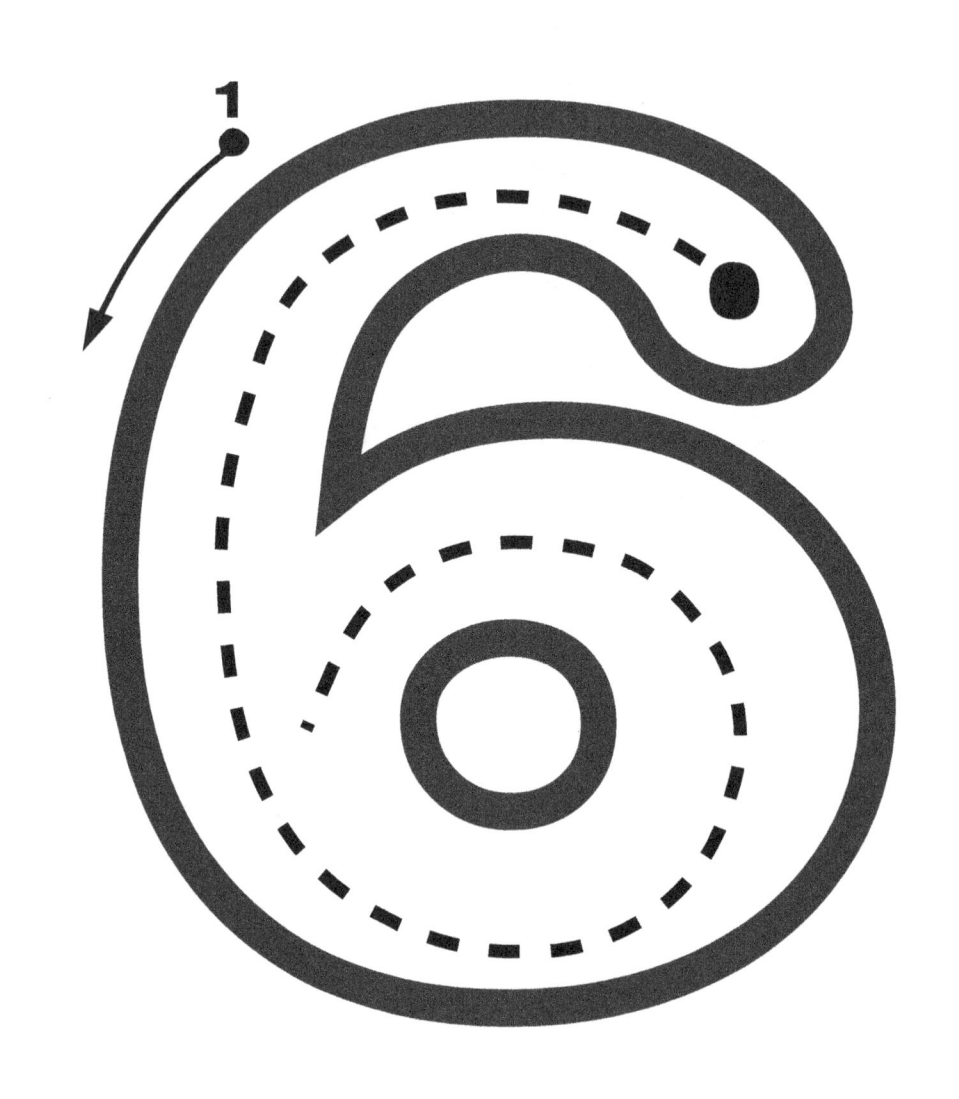

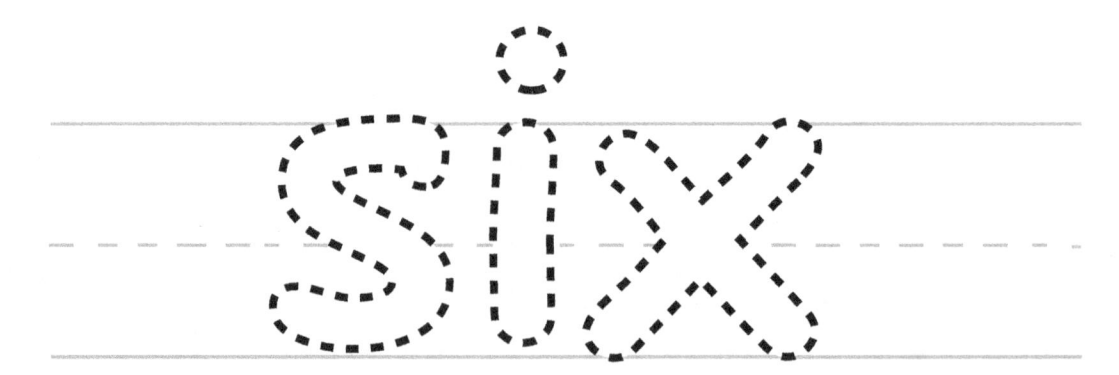

six

six

6

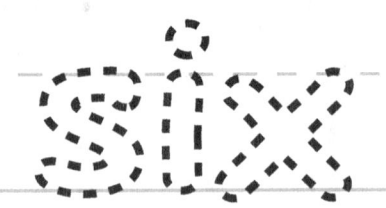

six six

six six six

six six six

6

6 6 6 6 6 6 6 6 6

7

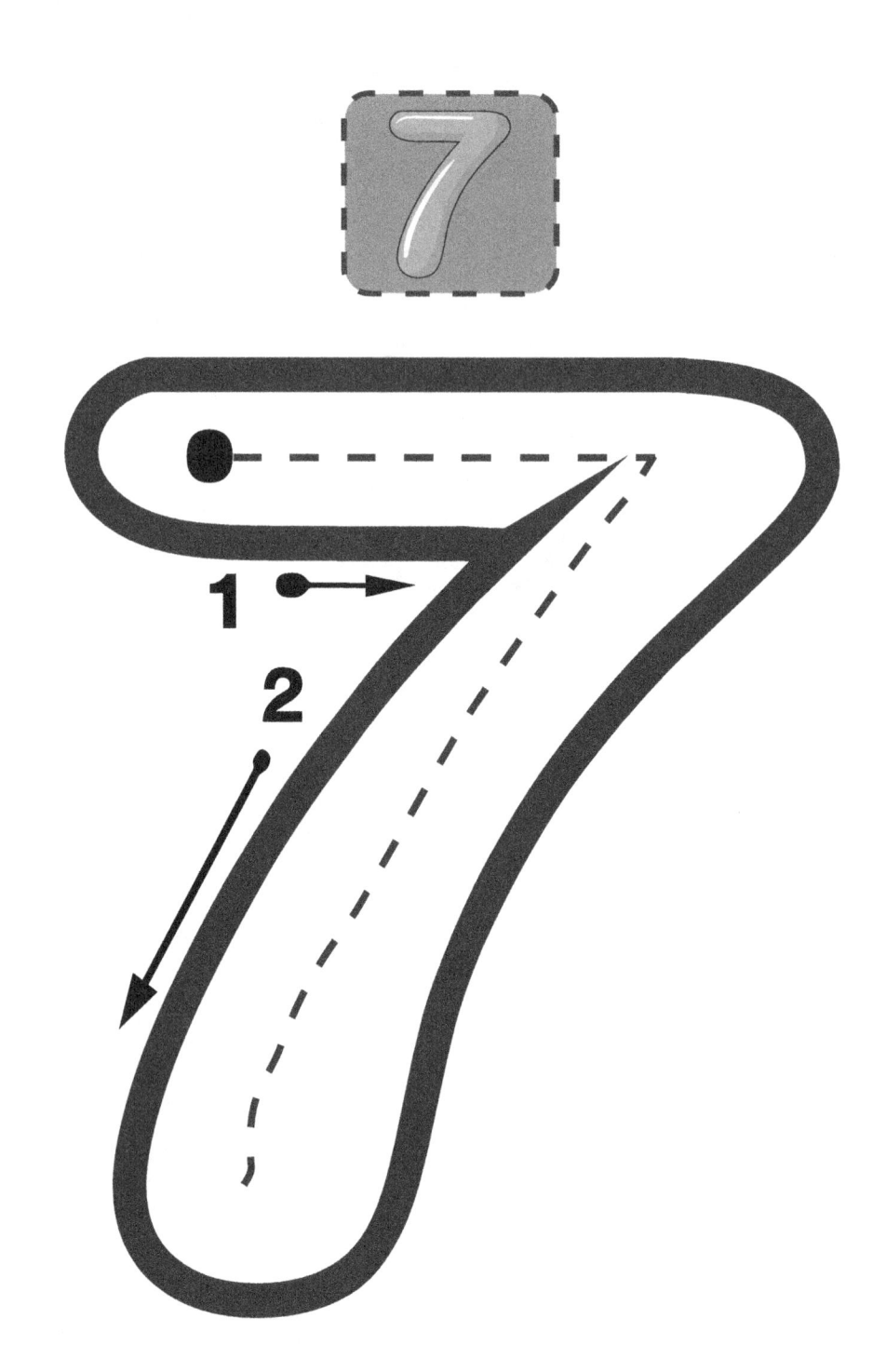

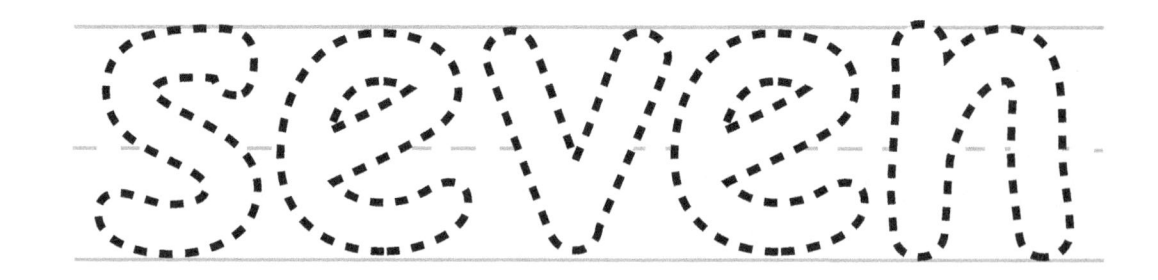

seven

seven

7

seven seven

seven seven

seven seven

7

8

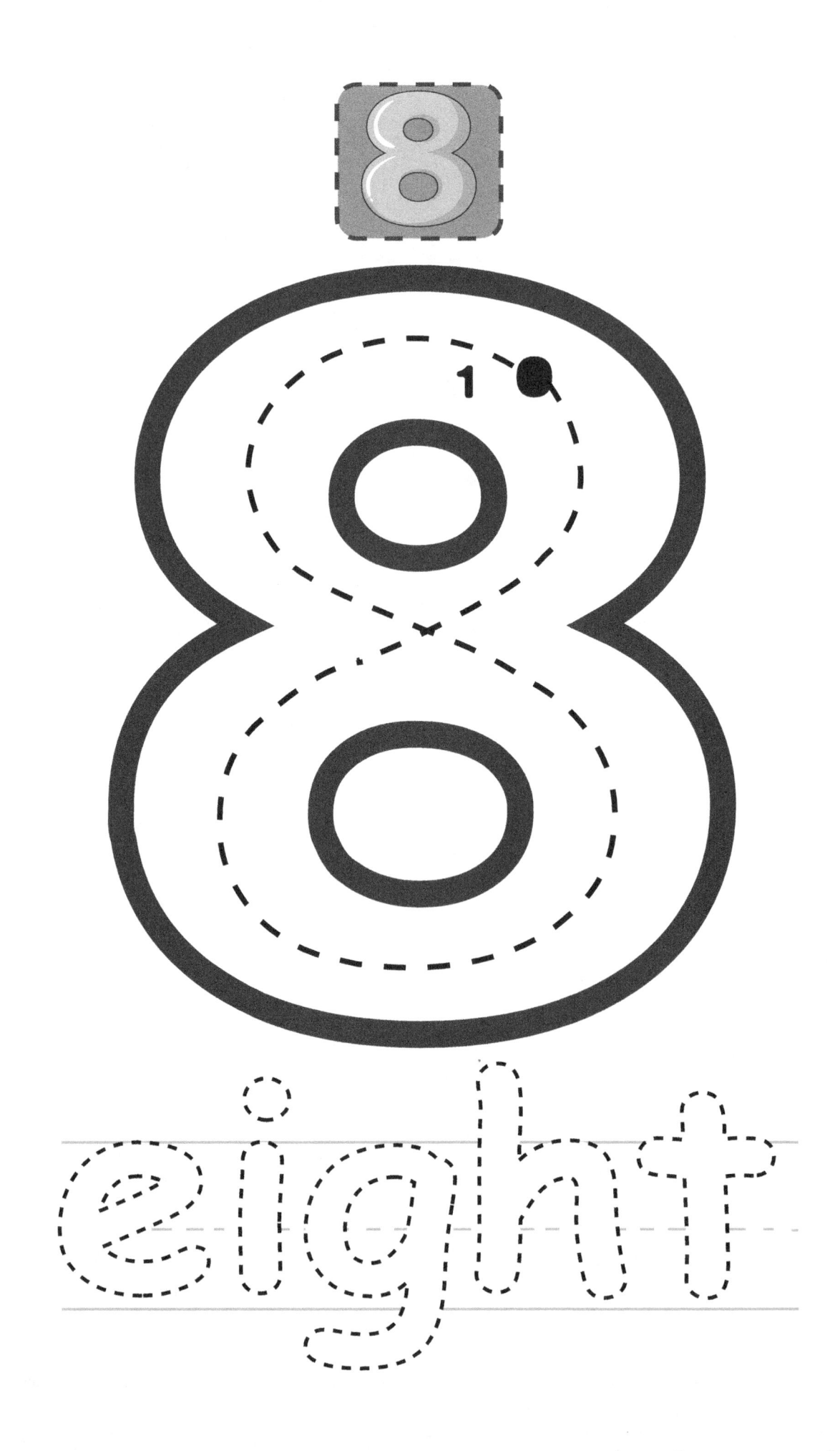

eight

eight

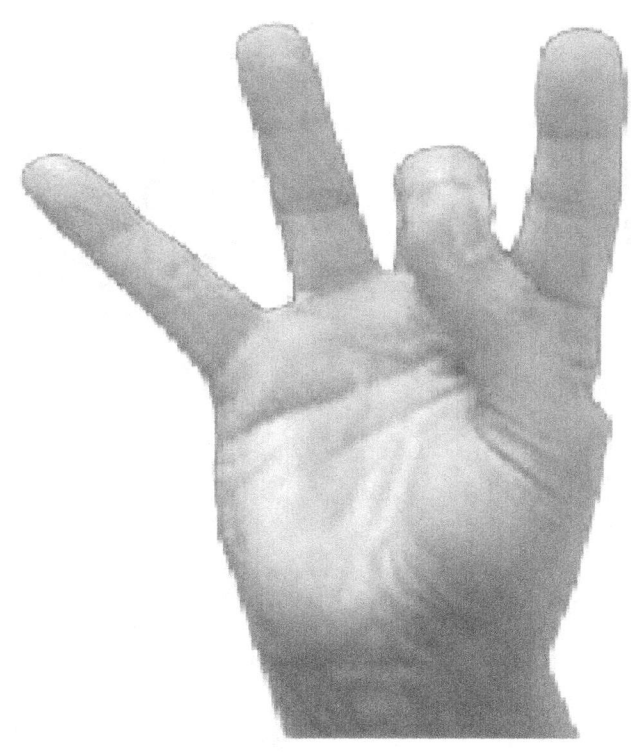

8

eight eight

eight eight

eight eight

8

8 8 8 8 8 8 8 8 8

9

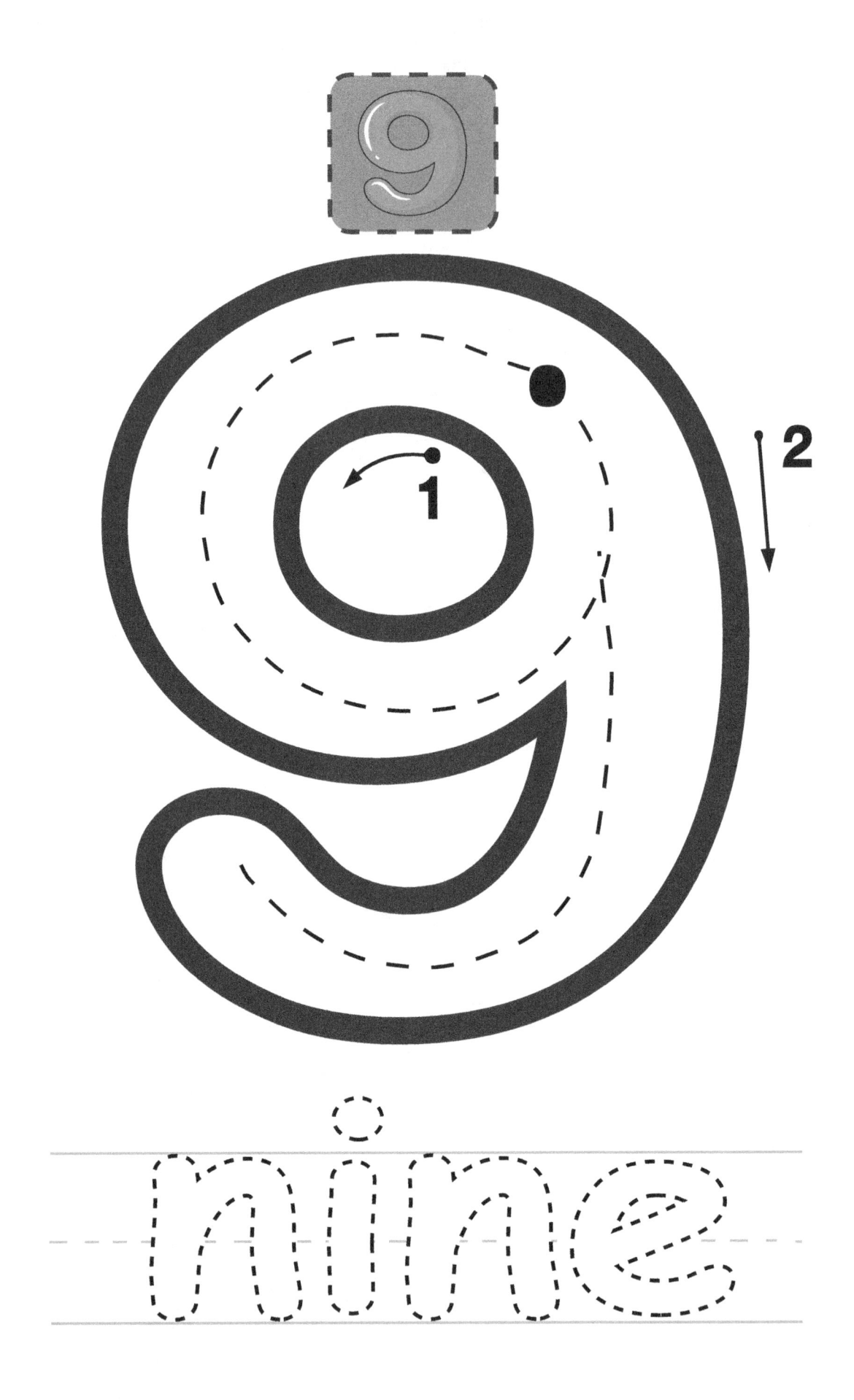

nine

nine

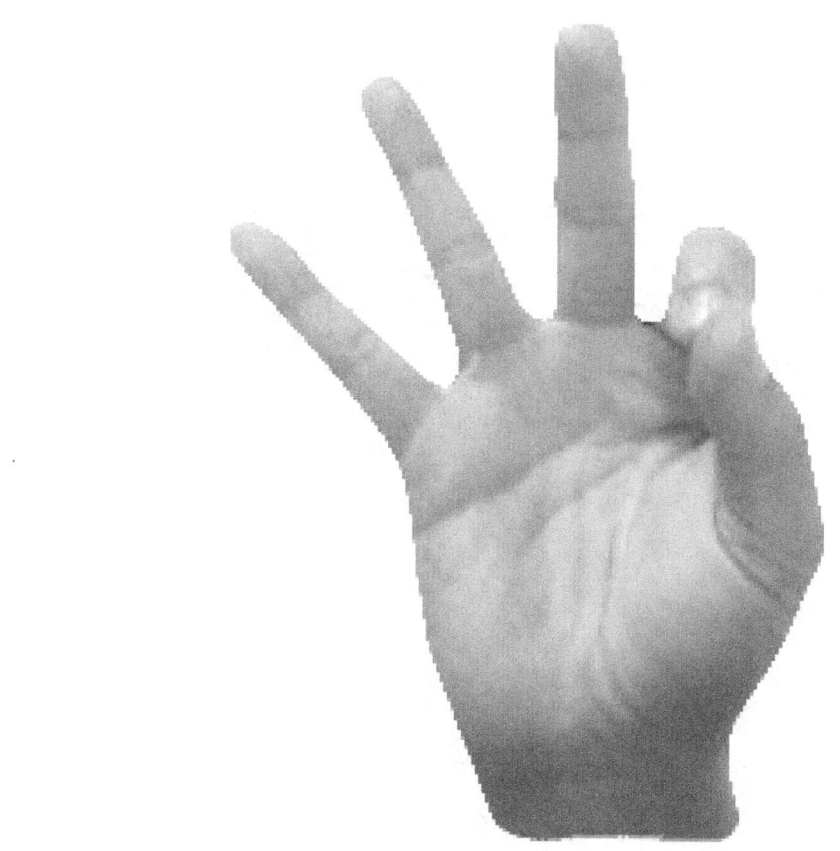

nine nine

nine nine

nine nine

9

q q q q q q q q q q q q

10

ten

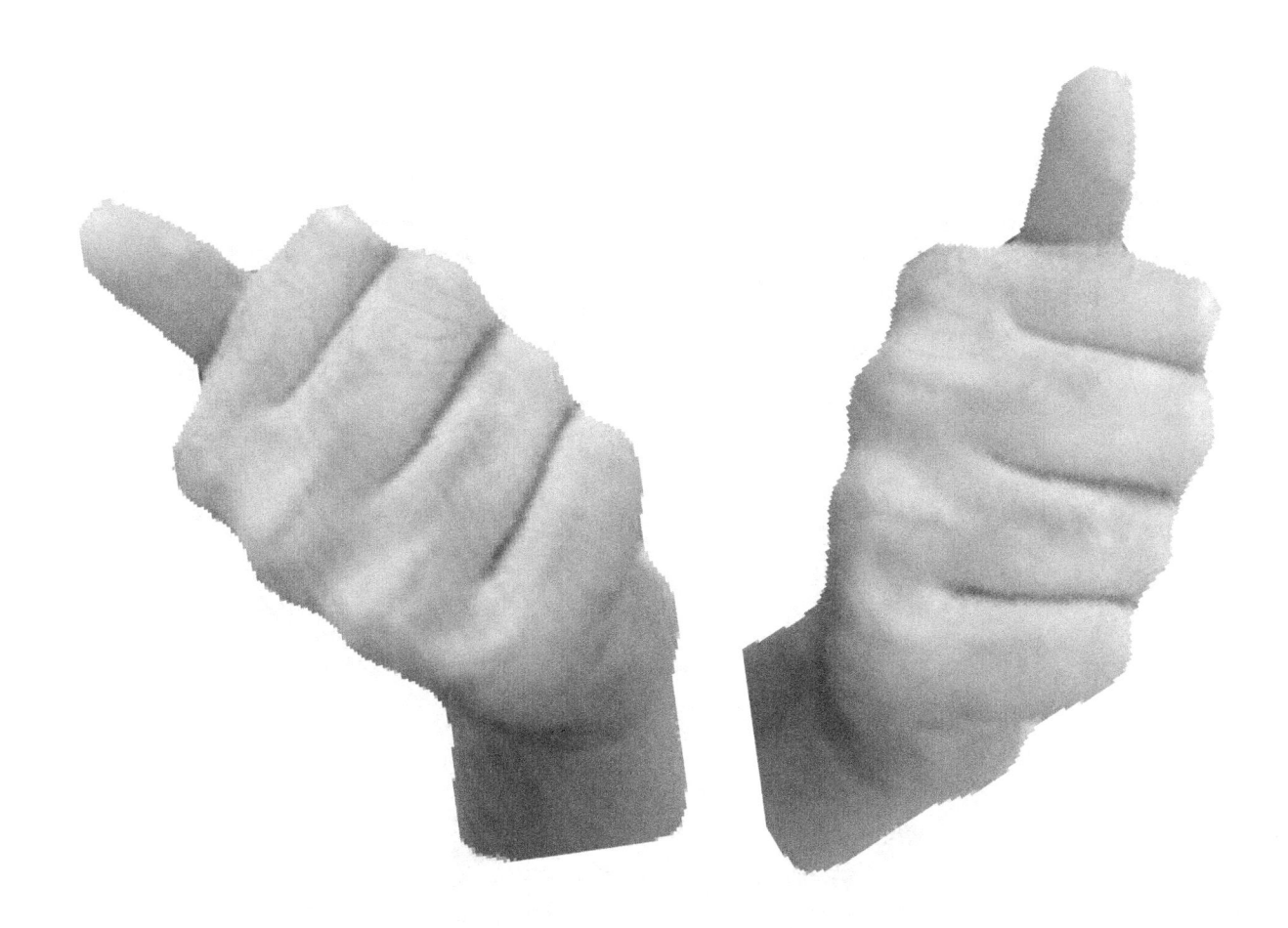

ten

10

ten ten

ten ten

ten ten

10

10 10 10 10 10 10 10

Made in the USA
Monee, IL
29 March 2025